FAMILY LIFE
Tudors & Stuarts

TESSA HOSKING

Wayland

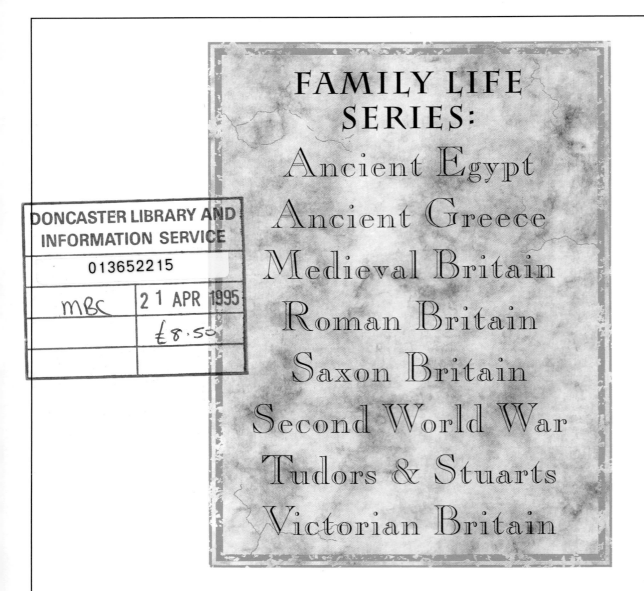

FAMILY LIFE
SERIES:

Ancient Egypt
Ancient Greece
Medieval Britain
Roman Britain
Saxon Britain
Second World War
Tudors & Stuarts
Victorian Britain

Series design: Pardoe Blacker Ltd
Editor: Katie Orchard
Production controller: Carol Stevens
Picture researcher: Liz Moore

First published in 1994 by Wayland (Publishers) Ltd
61 Western Road, Hove, East Sussex BN3 1JD, England

British Library Cataloguing in Publication Data
Hosking, Tessa
 Tudors and Stuarts. – (Family Life Series)
  I. Title II. Series
  941.05

ISBN 0 7502 1007 9

Printed and bound in Italy by Rotolito Lombarda S.p.A.

Cover pictures: Painting of the Saltonstall Family, and items found on the Mary Rose.

Picture acknowledgements: B T Batsford 11, 23 (top); The Bridgeman Art Library 18 © Copyright Tichborne Park, Hampshire, 24 top (Forbes Magazine Collections), 27 (top) © Copyright Wilton House, Wiltshire; Christ's Hospital Girls' School 15; English Heritage 22; E T Archive 28 (top); Hulton Deutsch 5 (top), 7 (top), 8, 9 (top), 14, 16 (bottom), 20 (top), 26 (middle), 27 (bottom), 28 (bottom); David MacLeod *back cover*; Mansell Collection 7 (bottom), 9 (bottom), 12; Mary Rose Trust *cover* (top); National Maritime Museum, London 24 and 25 (bottom); National Portrait Gallery 4, 19 (top); National Trust Photographic Library 21, 23 (bottom) © Copyright Lord Sackville; National Trust for Scotland 16 (top); Pepys Library, Cambridge 5 (bottom); Ryedale Folk Museum 10 (top); The Society of Antiquaries of London 19 (bottom); The Tate Gallery *cover* (centre) 20; Weidenfeld & Nicholson Archives 26 (top right). All artwork is by Peter Dennis.

CONTENTS

A CHANGING BRITAIN

James VI at the age of eight. James had been crowned king of Scotland in July 1567 when he was just over a year old.

This book is about family life in Britain under Tudor and Stuart (or Stewart) rule. The Tudor period in England began when Henry VII, the first Tudor monarch, **ascended** to the English throne in 1485. In 1603, his granddaughter, Queen Elizabeth I, died leaving no children. So the English crown passed to her great-nephew, the Stuart king, James VI of Scotland, who also became King James I of England. Stuart kings and queens had ruled in Scotland since 1371. The reign of the Stuarts ended with the death of Queen Anne in 1701. For nine years after the **execution** of Charles I in 1649, however, Britain was governed by Oliver Cromwell (1599–1658) and Parliament, and then for two years (from 1658 to 1660) by his son, Richard Cromwell.

A NEW AGE

During Tudor and Stuart rule, many important changes took place, both in Britain and abroad. International trade increased. Europeans **colonized** parts of Africa, Asia and America. There were new ideas about religion, art and science, and about how countries should be governed. The new middle-class felt that kings and queens had too much power. In Britain, some of these ideas led to **civil war** between 1642 and 1649. During the Tudor and Stuart period, the population of Britain nearly doubled. This led to food shortages, price rises and unemployment.

A father instructing his family in religion in 1563. Family prayer, and reading the Bible at home, were becoming common practices among Protestant families at this time.

THE
Gentlewomans Delight
IN
COOKERY.
32

Licenſed according to Order.

LONDON, Printed for *J. Back*, at the *Black*

Meanwhile, life in Britain was transformed into the early modern age. In fact, life for some families in Britain changed dramatically during the Tudor and Stuart period, for better or for worse, within their lifetimes.

By looking at the lives of families from different backgrounds, we are able in many cases to use written evidence left by the people themselves. Paintings, and pictures from printed books, show us how people looked and behaved. Houses, furniture, and other objects give us more clues to their everyday life.

*This kind of book was very popular with gentlewomen, and also with the wives of some rich farmers. They had become as well-off as the **gentry**, and wanted to live like them.*

5

FARMING FAMILIES

During the sixteenth and seventeenth centuries, most people in Britain lived and worked in the countryside. Some of them worked in industries such as mining or the manufacture of woollen cloth. Most people, however, spent their time farming the land. They produced food and raw materials for themselves, for the rest of the population, and for sale abroad.

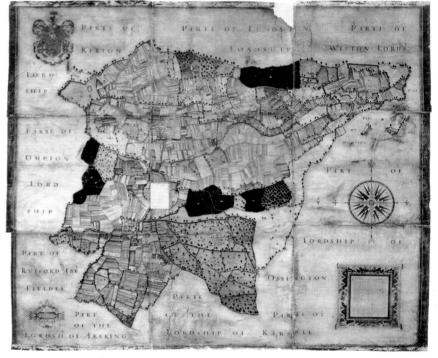

*This map of Laxton, Nottinghamshire (1635) shows the 'open field' system of farming. One field was left **fallow** each year, and animals grazed on it, so it recovered its goodness. A different crop was grown in each of the other fields each year.*

RICH AND POOR

Much of the land was owned by nobles and other rich landlords, who rented some of it out to farmers. Many farmers, however, owned their own land. Some of these farmers, often known as yeomen, became quite rich. The majority of farming families owned or rented only small farms, or were farm **labourers**. Many of these families were very poor.

The way that the land was divided up varied, but over much of Britain, villages were surrounded by three large 'open' fields. Each field was divided into strips, and the strips were shared out between the families of the village. So one family's land was often scattered in strips over the fields, and its animals were herded together with the other village animals. In such areas, it was difficult for good farmers to improve their land or add to their **livestock**.

A shepherd looking after sheep, from the Shepherd's Calendar *of 1579. The curved blade at one end of his crook might have been for cutting leaves for the sheep to eat, while the hook at the other end was for getting sheep out of awkward places.*

Over the years, therefore, many farmers exchanged land with one another, so that they could form larger plots which they could fence off or **enclose**. Some rich farmers and landlords enclosed a lot of their own land, and also **common land**. Small farmers were often evicted from their plots and homes. Often this was to make way for large flocks of sheep. Some of these farmers became farm labourers. Others, as the famous Tudor writer Thomas More put it:

'must depart, poor, wretched men, women, children, babes...
Away they trudge...finding no place to rest in...What can they else do but steal, and be hanged, or else go about begging?'

(Right) Members of a poor family, who probably had to leave their village when the land they farmed was enclosed. Many such families trudged from town to town in search of work.

FARM WORK

The lives of farming families revolved around work in the fields and around their homes. Everyone did what they could. Children as young as eight years old were given work to do. Rich farmers employed the children of poor farmers, who often worked as labourers until they had saved enough money to get married. At fourteen, children were expected to do adult jobs, and were paid adult wages. Women were paid less than men.

CROPS

In the fields, farmers grew wheat, rye, barley, oats, peas and beans. As these needed to be planted and looked after at different times of the year, there were always jobs to be done. While their father sowed wheat in the autumn, or barley in the spring, girls and boys scared away the birds with catapults. At haymaking and harvest time, in the early and late summer, the whole family had to join in to get the jobs done while there was still daylight.

Farmers worked from dawn until dusk, which of course meant longer hours in summer than in winter. They had breaks for meals, and in the summer they might have a nap at midday.

The front page of a sixteenth-century book on farming. Such books were popular among yeomen farmers, many of whom could read. Look at all the different farming jobs.

ANIMALS

The farmers kept animals including horses, cattle, sheep, pigs, rabbits, chickens, ducks and geese. Besides working or providing food, the animals were useful in other ways. Duck and goose feathers were used to fill soft, warm mattresses. Sheep were kept mainly for their wool, but also provided meat, manure, milk and more – as the old rhyme on the next page tells us:

'His tallow [fat] makes the candles white
To burne and serve us day and night...
His hornes some shepherds will not lose
Because with them they patch their shoes.'

*Villagers harvesting their landlord's corn. Men are cutting the corn with **sickles**, while women gather and tie it into **sheaves**.*

Sheep could stay outdoors all the time, guarded by a shepherd. Most other animals fed or grazed outdoors during the day, but were shut up safely at night. Children helped watch the animals as they grazed, or helped their mother look after young animals, feed chickens and collect eggs.

May Day was celebrated with fun and dancing. A May Queen and May King were chosen, and most people had the day off work. Shepherds, however, had to carry on minding the sheep.

A SMALL FARMING FAMILY'S HOME

The homes of farming families varied from one-room cottages to large, handsome farmhouses. In about 1650, the family of a small farmer was likely to live in a cottage with three ground-floor rooms: a **hall**, a **parlour** and a kitchen. The hall was open to the roof, but above the parlour was a loft which could be reached by a ladder. It was up here that the children slept, on straw-filled mattresses, surrounded by sacks of dried peas and bales (large bundles) of wool. Furniture was simple – a wooden table, some stools and one wooden bed. Spare clothes, bedding, wooden or **pewter** plates and spoons, and any money, were all stored in wooden chests. Behind the cottage were animal houses, a garden and some fruit trees.

(Above) A reconstructed thatched stone cottage in Yorkshire. The families of yeomen or better-off small farmers lived in homes like this, right through the Tudor and Stuart period.

10

A RICH YEOMAN'S HOME

The house of a rich yeoman's family was much bigger. When Alice Wheatley, a yeoman's widow, died in 1568, she left a house with a hall, two parlours, a kitchen, a **buttery**, a **larder** and three upstairs rooms. Around the house there were probably a barn, a stable, cowsheds and pigsties. There would also have been a dairy, a bakehouse and a brewery in which Alice supervised the making of butter, cheese, bread, and ale. Any of these not eaten by the household or farm labourers would have been taken to market to sell.

Inside a dairy belonging to a rich yeoman's family. The women are busy shaping cheeses and churning butter.

Alice would also have been in charge of the garden. William Harrison, a sixteenth-century writer, tells us that 'melons, pumpkins, cucumbers, radishes, parsnips, carrots, cabbages, turnips and all kinds of salad herbs' were commonly grown. In the orchard, there would have been apricots, apples, pears, plums, cherries and berries.

(Left) A reconstruction of the hall of a yeoman's farmhouse. Notice the open fire, pewter dishes and painted cloth on the wall.

The children of poor farmers hardly ever went to school, but those of yeomen sometimes did. A clever yeoman's son sometimes even went on to grammar school and university, in order to take up a career in the church, medicine or law.

11

TWO TOWN FAMILIES

During most of the sixteenth and seventeenth centuries, less than a tenth of the population of Britain lived in towns. Most towns were very small by our standards. The big exception was London, which in 1700 was the biggest city in Europe. Most of the richest merchants lived in London, but so did most of the poorest town labourers. In this chapter, however, we look at the lives of two families which were between these two extremes – and who lived in two very different towns.

Town children playing what looks like a game of Oranges and Lemons. Children also played outdoors with hoops, spinning-tops and balls.

THE SHAKESPEARES OF STRATFORD

Sixteenth-century Stratford was a medium-sized English market town. There were gardens and orchards among its few hundred houses, and behind the shops on its two main streets.

John Shakespeare was the son of a yeoman, but had moved to Stratford as a boy to learn a **trade**. After serving as an **apprentice** for seven years, he set up on his own as a glove maker. Once he was his own master, he could get married. Mary Arden, who married John in 1556, had inherited some property from her father, so the young couple could afford a large house in Stratford. John rose to become an important member of the town council.

A reconstruction of the Shakespeares' house in Henley Street, Stratford. A glove-shaped sign hangs outside John's shop, as many people could not read. The window-shutter lets down to make a display shelf.

Meanwhile, John carried on his trade in a workshop on the ground floor of their home. He made gloves from sheepskin and goatskin, and laid them out for sale just outside his workshop window. On Thursdays, he took a stall in the town market, and once or twice a year he may have sold more fashionable, expensive pairs of gloves at a fair.

The church record of the baptism of William Shakespeare. Written in Latin, part of the document translates: 'William, son of John Shakespeare'.

A scene in a grammar school in about 1600. Some boys are lining up to recite the Latin they have learned by heart. Notice how discipline is kept.

Mary's job was to run the home and look after their growing family. To help her, she must have had a servant girl, who lived and ate with them as one of the household. Sewing was an important job, as many of the family's clothes were made at home. Washing the clothes and household linen was very hard work, though it was not done as often as it is today. Houses were not cleaned as often, either. Dirt was trapped in rushes on the floor, and herbs were strewn around to cover up the bad smells.

John and Mary Shakespeare had eight children. Only five though, survived into adulthood, and only one, Joan, reached old age. This was not unusual, for many people died of illnesses which would now be prevented or cured.

Their first two daughters may have died in the **plague** of 1563–4. Their first son, however, who was only a baby then, survived it. He was William Shakespeare (1564–1616), who grew up to become the actor and playwright whose plays are still performed today.

All the children may have attended a 'little' school where they learned to read and write. Only the boys went on to grammar school, where they learned to read and write Latin. Their school day lasted from seven o'clock in the morning until five or six o'clock in the evening, with a two-hour break at midday. The girls, meanwhile, stayed at home to help with the housework and learn all the skills they would need to become housewives themselves.

At five o'clock in the afternoon, John shut up the shop, the children came home from school, and Mary put supper on the table. After they had eaten, John hung a lantern outside the house to light the street, and Mary put the **dole-cupboard** out for passing **vagrants** to help themselves.

THE GLADSTONES OF EDINBURGH

In the seventeenth century, Edinburgh, the capital of Scotland, was still a walled city. Sloping down from its castle was the 'Kings Hie Street', lined on both sides by tall stone and timber buildings, known as 'lands'. In December 1617, one of these 'lands' was bought by Thomas Gledstanes (now spelt Gladstone) and his wife, Bessie Cunningham. Thomas was one of the many merchants in Edinburgh who traded with foreign countries.

There were some girls' schools, though many taught mainly skills such as needlework. Christ's Hospital was one of the charity schools for both boys and girls. Founded in 1552, it still exists today. Here we see the Tudor girls' uniform in its original colours.

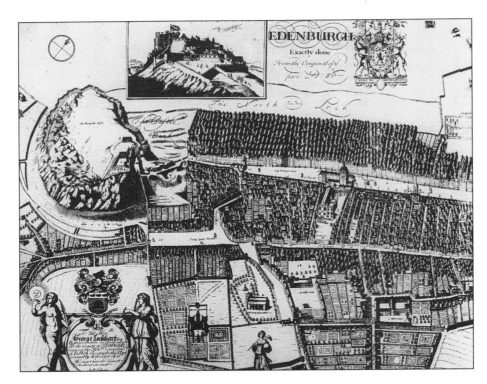

A map of Edinburgh in 1647, showing 'Gladstone's land'. Notice how packed the houses in 'The Hie Street' are compared with those further south, which have long back gardens.

As soon as they bought their new property, Thomas and Bessie set about extending it. A large new room was added at the front on each of the floors, extending the property twenty-three feet (just over seven metres) into the 'Kings Hie Street'. Living space in the city was so valuable that no one lived in a whole 'land'. So, Thomas and Bessie lived on their third floor, and let out the rest of the property to tenants.

The ground floor was let as two **booths**, or shops. One probably sold Scottish-made goods, such as wool and linen woven cloth, coloured with natural dyes like gorse and heather. The other may have sold imported goods such as tobacco, sugar-candy, prunes and ginger. In the cellar below was a **tavern**. The upper floors were let as self-contained flats. The higher the flat, the less expensive it was.

The new front room of the Gladstones' flat was their hall, and they had it decorated in the latest style. The wooden ceiling was colourfully painted with birds, leaves and flowers. Along the top of the

An apothecary's (chemist's) shop in Holland in 1661. Such shops only existed in large towns. There were probably such shops in Edinburgh. Housewives usually had to make up their own herbal remedies for many ailments.

16

stone wall was a border, painted grey, rust and yellow, and below this, linen hangings painted in green, rust and gold. The furniture was of heavy, dark oak: a table, four chairs and a huge, carved cupboard. In the corner was their proudest possession – a carved oak four-poster bed, hung with bright curtains. After dark, the room was lit by six candles in a plain wrought-iron candelabra. As well as sleeping and eating in this room, the Gladstones entertained visitors, Bessie sewed, Thomas planned his business dealings, and their four young daughters were allowed to play if they behaved themselves!

From the hall, one door led to the girls' bedroom. Another led to the kitchen, which was where the family's two servant girls slept. They had to help with all the housework, including fetching water in buckets, and spinning linen and woollen yarn on the spinning-wheel.

A reconstruction of the Gladstones' kitchen, in which cooking was done over the open fire. Notice the pull-out servants' bed, the baby's cradle and baby-walker. The light on the wall was called a cruisie lamp, and the 'pattens' (a type of shoe) in front of the fire were to keep their wearer's feet out of the dirt in the streets outside.

THE NOBILITY AND GENTRY

The **nobility** and gentry were the upper classes of Tudor and Stuart Britain. We know more about their lives than those of most other people of this period. One reason is that some of them wrote their own accounts of their lives. Two very different people who did this were the gentleman John Dee and the noblewoman Lady Anne Clifford.

*The Tichborne **Dole**. Sir Henry Tichborne and his family, surrounded by their large household, are giving a dole of bread to all their farm labourers.*

JOHN DEE'S FAMILY

John Dee was a mathematician, astronomer and astrologer. In January 1577, he started to keep a diary about both his work and his personal life. The next year, he married Jane Fromond, who was a **lady-in-waiting** at the court of Queen Elizabeth. John was fifty years old and Jane was only twenty-two, but they became a happy couple. Of their eight children, only two died in childhood as far as we know. Their home was in Mortlake, on the River Thames in London, but John's work took the family abroad for long stretches of time.

BIRTH AND BABYHOOD

In these diary entries, John Dee records the important events in the early years of his first two children. The diaries show that the children were breast-fed by **wet-nurses**. This was usual among the nobility and gentry. Sometimes babies went to stay at their wet-nurse's homes until they were **weaned** or longer, and sometimes, as we see, the wet-nurses came to stay with them.

1579 **July**
13 Arthur Dee born.
16 Arthur was christened.

1580 **January**
16 Arthur fell sick with cold...could not sleep, eat or drink.

August
27 Arthur was weaned.
30 Wet-Nurse Darant was discharged [sent away].

1581 **June**
7 Katherine Dee was born.
10 Katherine christened.

August
4 Katherine was sent home from Nurse Maspely of Barnes for fear of her maid's sickness, and Goodwife Benet gave her suck.

1582 **August**
8 Kate [Katherine] was sickly.
25 Katherine was taken home from Nurse Garet and weaned.

(Above) Sir Henry Unton as a baby, in the arms of his mother, Lady Anne Seymour. Behind them his wet-nurse waits to lay him in his cradle.

The baby of a well-to-do family being christened in 1624. Babies were christened within days of being born, as it was very common for them to die of illnesss or infection. It was believed that if they were not baptized, they would not go to Heaven.

PLAY

Sometimes, like today, children played at make-believe. Sometimes, as these diary extracts show, their games ended in accidents.

1582 January
    22 Arthur Dee and Mary Herbert did make a show of childish marriage, calling each other husband and wife.

1590 August
    5 Rowland fell into the Thames over head and ears.

1591 June
    27 At Mr Herbert's, Arthur wounded on his head by his own throwing of brickbat, and not well avoiding it.

These are the sorts of games that John Dee's children would have played with their friends.

DISCIPLINE

The rather puzzling entry below, gives us a glimpse of the kind of strict discipline which most parents believed was right for their children. Most people thought it was all right to beat children.

1589 May
    21 Katherine, by a blow on the ear given by her mother, did bleed at the nose very much.

A noble family in about 1640. The father has brought his son and daughter to see the new baby. Their mother looks very weak. Unfortunately, women often died from infections after childbirth.

EDUCATION

When Arthur was eight and Katherine was six, a tutor was hired to teach them Latin. Later, they had a schoolmaster called Mr Lee. When she was nearly nine, however, Katherine went to live with and be taught by Mistress Brayce at Brentford, London. When Arthur was nearly thirteen, he was sent to Westminster School. Lastly, in 1596, 'Mary Goodwyn came to govern and teach the younger daughters.' It would be interesting to know what John Dee's children were taught besides the main subjects of Latin and Greek, because we know that the children of well-educated parents often also learnt arithmetic, astronomy, music, modern languages, history and geography. Most girls were not educated as highly as boys, but they also had to learn the skills of needlecraft and household management.

A sixteenth-century embroidered cushion cover showing a noble family in their garden. Young men are catching birds, while the lady admires some fruit. This embroidery comes from Hardwick Hall in Derbyshire.

THE FAMILY OF LADY ANNE CLIFFORD

The English nobility, into which Lady Anne Clifford was born, lived lives of wealth and splendour. Families moved from one of their mansions or castles to another, taking with them huge households, and nearly all their furniture and belongings. Family members often lived apart. Sometimes parents sent their children to live with friends or relatives.

Lady Anne Clifford was born in 1590, the daughter of the Earl and Countess of Cumberland. She married Richard Sackville, Earl of Dorset, when they were both nineteen. Their first child, Margaret, was born on 2 July 1614. They then had three sons, but all of them died as babies. Their fifth child, Isabella, was born in 1622.

Lady Anne kept a diary for most of her long life, although much of it is now lost. Part of that which survives covers the years 1616 to 1619. During these years, Margaret was still an only child, and her mother recorded the important moments in her growing up, as these extracts show. Notice that she is usually called simply 'the child'.

SOME WORRYING TIMES

Children's illnesses were very worrying for their parents, since they could so easily be fatal. Rich people could afford to send for a doctor, but their medicines were often no better than the herbal remedies that poorer people relied on.

Richard Sackville, Earl of Dorset, probably at about the time that he married Lady Anne.

1616 January

22 *The child had a fit of the **ague** in the morning. Mr Smith went in the coach to London to my Lord [husband] to let him know how she was. . . he came down to see her.*
23 *The Lord went up to London again.*
25 *I spent most of my time in working [embroidery] and in going up and down [to and from the nursery] to see the child.*

February

21 *The child had a fit of the ague and the doctor gave her a salt powder to put in her beer.*

SIGNS OF GROWING UP

Lady Anne recorded in her diary those events which marked her daughter's growing up. Some of these things are still familiar to families today.

1616 March

    11 *The child had two great teeth come out so that she now had eighteen.*

    April

    28 *The first time the child put on a whalebone bodice.*

    May

    1 *I cut the child's strings off from her coats to get her used to walking on her own. She had two or three falls at first but was not hurt.*

1619 June

    4 *This night was the first that Lady Margaret lay alone, Maria [her nanny] having a bed made close by.*

Lady Margaret Sackville, daughter of Lady Anne Clifford, aged four or five. Notice her very grown-up clothes and hair.

Noble children playing in the seventeenth century. Although Margaret was an only child until she was eight, she probably played like this with the children of family friends.

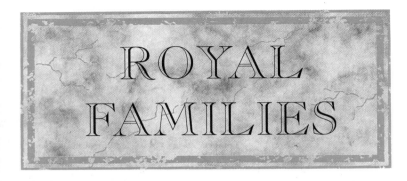

ROYAL FAMILIES

Henry VIII visiting his son, Prince Edward, in his nursery in 1538. Five-year-old Princess Elizabeth can be seen on the left. This picture was painted in Victorian times.

Royal families led lives unlike those of any other people, for they followed both the tastes and fortunes of the monarch, as we shall see.

HENRY VIII AND HIS CHILDREN

No matter how magnificent a monarch he became, Henry VIII would have been considered a failure if he had not had a son to succeed him. That was why he divorced his first wife, Catherine of Aragon, and had his second wife, Anne Boleyn, beheaded. Catherine had six babies over the years she and Henry were married, but only one of them, Mary, survived. Anne Boleyn had only a daughter, Elizabeth. Henry's third wife, Jane Seymour, gave birth to a son, Edward. He survived, but only twelve days later, Jane died. Henry married again three times, but had no more children.

Each of his wives and children were given houses of their own, as well as **lodgings** in his grandest houses. At Hampton Court, for instance, new lodgings were built for Prince Edward. He had a day nursery, a rocking chamber (bedroom), lavatory, bathroom and kitchen. His sisters' accommodation had varied according to their mothers' fortunes. After Mary's mother's divorce, for instance, a foreign ambassador wrote that:

> *'the king has caused the princess to dislodge from a very fine house to a very inferior one.'*

Two months later, Mary was told to move again, this time to join her half-sister's household. Worse had happened two years earlier, however, when Mary was fifteen. Up until then she had nearly always lived with her mother. Then Henry suddenly told them that they must live separately. Later on, Mary was forbidden to even write to her mother.

Henry had been very fond and proud of both his daughters when they were little. They were given an excellent education by the very best of teachers. So too, of course, was their brother, Edward.

It was only after Henry had married his sixth wife, however, that his three children lived together much in the same house. Catherine Parr took a real interest in her step-children. Mary was grown up by then, but Elizabeth was still only ten, and Edward was six. Three years later, Henry died. His son became king, to be followed to the throne in turn by his eldest sister Mary, and then Elizabeth.

On the left of this picture is the Tudor palace at Greenwich, where Princess Mary was born in 1516, and in which all three of Henry's children had lodgings.

MARY QUEEN OF SCOTS AND HER SON JAMES

Mary became Queen of Scotland in 1543 when she was only a few days old. At five and a half, she was **betrothed** to the heir of the French throne, and sent to live at the French court. She married at fifteen, but two years later her young husband Francis fell ill and died. Mary wrote in a poem:

'I feel the deepest sadness...[for] He who was my dearest.'

An imaginary portrait of Mary Queen of Scots and her son, James. In fact, they were never together after he was ten months old.

(Above) A letter written to Mary by her son James when he was twelve years old. It is signed at the bottom by his tutor.

Mary had little more happiness in life. Back in Scotland, she fell in love with and married Henry, Lord Darnley in 1565. Two years later, however, he was murdered.

Their son, James, was born in June 1566. When he was three months old, Mary left him in the care of his own household at Stirling Castle, the traditional home of Scottish royal babies. She visited him whenever she could, but she had to carry out her royal duties. Soon, Mary had many enemies. This was partly because she had remained a Catholic, while others with power in Scotland had become Protestant. In June 1567, she was taken prisoner, and forced to **abdicate** in favour of her son. James was brought up as a Protestant so that Scotland could have a Protestant king.

Meanwhile, Mary was held prisoner, first in Scotland and then in England, until she was executed twenty years later. She wrote her son many letters, and sent him gifts. The last time that she saw him, however, was when he was only ten months old.

THE FAMILY OF CHARLES I

King Charles and Henrietta Maria were a devoted married couple. They had eight children: Charles, Mary, James, Elizabeth, Anne, Catherine, Henry and Henrietta.

The first seven children spent most of their early years in St. James's Palace in London. When Charles was born there in 1630, his nursery was staffed by a wet-nurse, nurse, **governess** and six ladies to rock his cradle. As the children grew, they played with the children of **courtiers** in the fine rooms and beautiful gardens of the palace. Governesses taught them to read, write and behave properly. They did not see much of their parents, who were usually busy elsewhere.

At the age of eight, Charles, as heir to the throne, was provided with his own court at Richmond. An earl was put in charge of his education. Good manners and horsemanship were considered very important. When he started to go with his father to watch what happened in Parliament, however, he discovered the more serious side of his royal position, for disagreement between the King and Parliament was coming to a head. In 1642, civil war began between **Royalists** and **Parliamentarians**. The happy and secure life led by the royal children came to a sudden end.

The three eldest children of Charles I: Charles, James and Mary. James (centre) has not yet reached the age when boys were 'breeched' (put into trousers).

Charles I, with servants and several members of his family, on the river at Hampton Court.

FOOD

The food eaten by people in Tudor and Stuart times differed, like everything else, between the different classes in society.

ROYAL AND NOBLE FAMILIES

Royal families – even sometimes each member of a royal family – had private kitchens where meals were prepared just for them and their chosen guests. Even if the king or queen was eating alone, he or she was served with great ceremony. Dozens of dishes of meat, sauces and **sweetmeats** were brought in, from which he or she could choose. The rest of the court – sometimes hundreds of nobles, gentlemen and ladies – were catered for by great kitchens like those which can still be seen at Hampton Court.

When in their own homes, noble families usually ate in their private dining-rooms. On special occasions, however, family and guests joined the household servants in the hall. Then dinner, which was usually served at 11 am, or supper, which was served at 5 or 6 pm, became a feast lasting up to two or three hours. Sometimes, the feast would be rounded off with a banquet, which was a dessert course made up of some decorative **sweetmeats**, fruit and wine.

Lord and Lady Cobham, their six children and the children's aunt, eating dessert off silver plates. The children are wearing their best clothes and jewellery, which were very fashionable for the year 1567.

WORKING FAMILIES

Working families in towns or in the country sat down to family meals three times a day if they could afford to. An early breakfast of bread, eggs or porridge, with milk or ale, prepared them for the morning's work. Town families met again to eat at midday. Craftsmen shut up shop and children came home from school for dinner, which had been cooked over the open fire in the kitchen. Roast and boiled meat, pies, home-grown vegetables, fruit and tarts were washed down with beer, ale or wine. A similar but lighter meal was served as supper at the end of the day.

A painting by an Italian artist showing preparations for a noble feast. Beyond the kitchen, the guests can be seen gathering in the hall.

FARMING FAMILIES

Farming families often ate their midday meal in the fields, so it was simply ale or cider with bread and cheese, or a pasty. Supper was their main cooked meal, eaten when the day's work was done. A poor family usually had **pottage** and bread, with fish or bacon if they were lucky. The families of yeomen could usually look forward to a simple but large supper made up of roast meats, **puddings** and pies.

During the seventeenth century, new flavours and methods of cooking became increasingly popular. New foods and dishes were introduced from France, Italy, and as far away as Turkey and Persia (modern-day Iran) as explorers found new countries with different types of food. New recipe books were published every few years. Fashions in food, as in most things, started with the royal family and worked their way down the social scale. Most ordinary families, however, continued with their plain and simple food, and lives, to the end of the Tudor and Stuart period and beyond.

GLOSSARY

Abdicate To give up the throne.

Ague A type of fever.

Apprentice A person learning a skilled job, by working in return for training.

Ascended Became king.

Betrothed Engaged to be married.

Booths Small shops with shutters at the front.

Buttery Store for wine or ale.

Civil war A war between people of the same country.

Colonized Settled in a new area and established a community there.

Common land Land which could be used by everyone in the village.

Courtier A noble person living at the royal court.

Dole A charitable gift of food, clothes or money.

Dole-cupboard A cupboard in which left over food was stored before being given to the poor.

Enclose To fence or otherwise close off a piece of land for private use.

Execution Killing someone as a punishment.

Fallow To have no crops growing on it.

Gentry Families of gentlemen, not quite nobility.

Governess A woman who is paid to teach children in their homes.

Labourers People who do physical work for wages.

Lady-in-waiting A personal maid, dedicatated to the comfort of a lady noble.

Larder A cool room for storing meat and fresh food.

Livestock Animals reared to provide food.

Lodgings Private rooms which were rented.

Nobility Titled people such as lords and ladies.

Parliamentarians During the civil war, they were the people who supported Oliver Cromwell.

Parlour A private room in a house, usually used for sleeping in.

Pewter A mixture of metals (mostly tin) used to make plates and other tableware.

Plague A very serious infectious disease, spread by the fleas that live on rats.

Pottage Thick soup.

Puddings Meat, fruit or vegetables mixed with flour and other ingredients and boiled in a cloth.

Royalists During the civil war, they were the people who supported King Charles I.

Sheaves Bundles of corn stalks tied together at harvest time.

Sickles Tools used for cutting. It has a curved blade and a short handle.

Sweetmeats A special type of sweetened cake.

Tavern A public house, similar to a pub today.

Trade The selling of a particular type of goods.

Vagrants Wandering, homeless people.

Weaned Learnt to eat solid food.

Wet-nurses Women whose job it is to breast-feed another woman's baby.

BOOKS TO READ

Chrisp, Peter, *Food*, Tudors and Stuarts series (Wayland, 1993)

Frost, Abigail, *Elizabeth I*, Children of History series (Cherrytree Books, 1989)

Honey, Alison, *Investigating the Tudors* (The National Trust, 1993)

Purkis, Sallie, *Tudor and Stuart Life* (Longman, 1992)

Shuter, Jane; Hook, Adam and Maguire, Judith, *Tudor and Stuart Times* (Heinemann Educational, 1992)

Triggs, Tony D, *Town Life* and *Country Life*, Tudors and Stuarts series (Wayland, 1993)

Triggs, Tony D, *Tudor Britain*, History in Evidence series (Wayland, 1989)

PLACES TO VISIT

Dorney Court, Dorney, near Windsor, Berkshire, England.
A very handsome Tudor manor house, which has been inhabited by the same family for 400 years.

Gladstone's Land, High Street, Edinburgh, Scotland.
A seventeenth-century merchant's house, with shop booths on the ground floor, furnished and fitted in period.

Hardwick Hall, near Chesterfield, Derbyshire, England.
A very big and grand house built by Elizabeth, Countess of Shrewsbury, in the late sixteenth century. Especially fine collection of tapestries and needlework, and long gallery containing eighty-one pictures.

Plas Mawr (Great Mansion), High Street, Conway, Gwynedd, Wales.
A fine Tudor town house, containing many interesting and unspoilt features.

Rydale Folk Museum, Hutton le Hole, Yorkshire, England.
Reconstructed farmhouses, including those of the sixteenth and seventeenth centuries, equipped and furnished to give a feel of everyday country life.

Traquair House, Innerleithen, Peebleshire, Scotland.
'The oldest inhabited house in Scotland'. Visited by Mary, Queen of Scots, in 1566, it contains several of her possessions among its many Stuart artefacts.

Welsh Folk Museum, St Fagans, near Cardiff, South Glamorgan, Wales.
Reconstructed farmhouses and farm buildings, including those of the sixteenth and seventeenth centuries, furnished and equipped to illustrate the life and culture of Wales.

INDEX